FOREW

"It is time for parents to teach young people early on that in diversity, there is beauty, and there is strength." ~ Maya Angelou

I could hear a cat meowing loudly in the background during what turned out to be one of the last telephone conversations I had with my younger brother, Brad, a 30-year veteran of the Los Angeles Police Department, who was diagnosed with cancer around the time of his birthday in November 2019. When I asked who was making all the racket, he told me it was "Sookie," a cat in his menagerie of three cats and three dogs. He told me that Sookie was particularly empathetic and provided soothing companionship throughout his difficult recovery from chemotherapy and radiation therapy. He went on to tell me that Sookie has a distinctive physical characteristic - polydactylism - that greatly fascinated me and inspired this book.

It's a well-known fact that the writer, Ernest Hemingway, had a particular affinity for polydactyl cats and had a few of them sharing his home in Key West, Florida (now a museum and a refuge for some of the descendants of his cherished pets). To this day, polydactyl cats are sometimes referred to as "Hemingway cats," as well as "thumb cats," "mitten cats," etc. The Guinness World Records cites two cats as having a total of 28 fully functioning toes (each with a pad and claw – irrespective of the thumb-like "dewclaw" on a cat's inner forelegs). That's seven toes on each paw!

This discovery immediately became the catalyst (no pun intended) for "The Cat With Twenty Toes," using Sookie as a metaphor for the broad spectrum of physical differences among living creatures. There's nothing "wrong" with Sookie. She's just a little different than most other cats, which is what makes her interesting. When we see an elephant, for example, we accept and are not judgmental of its large ears, trunk, tusks, and other distinctive physical characteristics. Why, I wondered, couldn't we be just as accepting and non-judgmental of people whose physical characteristics are different than our own?

That's the essence of "The Cat With Twenty Toes." I hope it's successful in imparting a message to readers that celebrates our many physical differences and encourages diversity.

My brother succumbed to cancer in October 2020. He was short in stature, but had a huge heart and treated everyone with respect and dignity. We could use more like him these days. ~ TL

Brad and Sookie.

The author gratefully acknowledges the following individuals, whose generous contributions helped make this book possible:

Izzy Bean
Doug and Nonie Beal
Ed Becker and Associates

The Cat With Twenty Toes

Written by Tony Lovitt

Illustrated by Izzy Bean

We have a cat named Sookie.
She has twenty toes.
How Sookie got four extra,
no one really knows.

She walks just fine, and we're in awe.
She has five toes on every paw!

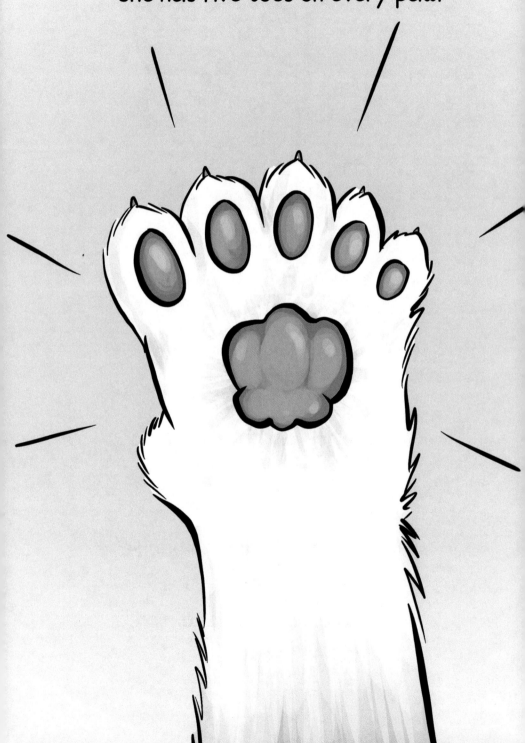

She'll roll on her back
and strike a pose.
She loves to show off
all those toes.

she takes along

all those toes.

It's a good thing cats
don't wear shoes.
Her feet would make
the evening news!

Sookie has no extra parts,
except for those spare toes.
After all, what would she do
if she had one more nose?

It's no big deal.
Our feet have five toes, too.
Maybe we need six?
Do we have too few?

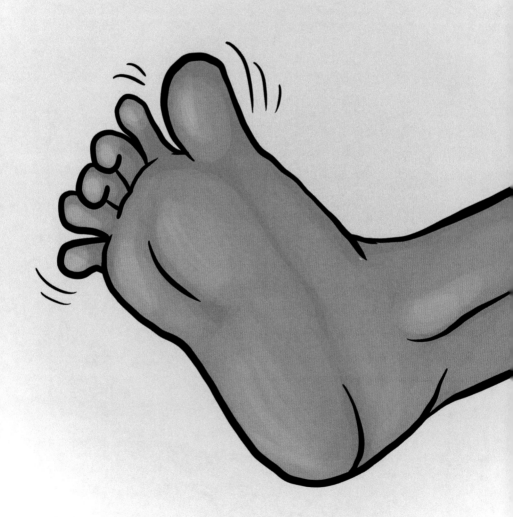

Each and every night,
as we begin to doze...
...we count sheep.
She counts her toes.

She's as sweet as honey.
Sookie wouldn't hurt a fly.
If a bird flew near her,
she wouldn't even sigh.

But,
we don't dare let her venture out.
We keep all doors closed.
Outside's far too dangerous
for our cat with twenty toes!

Whether in sunshine or rain,

or whenever it snows...

...Sookie's our friend

and our love only grows.

Sure, our Sookie's different.
But, aren't we all?
Our differences make us special,
whether we're big or small.

Moose have great big antlers.

Elephants have long trunks.

Some camels have two humps.

And then there are
the skunks.

Whales live in deep water.
Eagles, they go soaring.
If everyone were the same,
it would surely be boring.

Some have scales and some have fur.
Some have fins or feathers.
No matter what's on someone's outside,
we all need to get along together.

So, it's great our cat is different
and, just so everybody knows...
...we'll always love our Sookie,
the cat with twenty toes.

Made in the USA
Middletown, DE
13 November 2021